D1553429

The LITTLE
BOOK *of*
COURAGE

Also by Barbara Lewis Marco

Stumbling Toward Enlightenment:
An Illustrated Companion

The LITTLE
BOOK *of*
COURAGE

An Illustrated Guide to Challenging Our Fears

BARBARA LEWIS MARCO

**Andrews McMeel
Publishing**

Kansas City

For My Son, Jesse

The Little Book of Courage copyright © 2003 by Barbara Lewis Marco. Some images © 2003 www.clipart.com. All rights reserved. Printed in Hong Kong. No part of this book may be used or reproduced in any manner whatsoever without written permission except in the case of reprints in the context of reviews. For information, write Andrews McMeel Publishing, an Andrews McMeel Universal company, 4520 Main Street, Kansas City, Missouri 64111.

03 04 05 06 07 KFO 10 9 8 7 6 5 4 3 2 1

ISBN: 0-7407-3848-8

Library of Congress Catalog Control Number: 2003101276

Attention: Schools and Businesses

Andrews McMeel books are available at quantity discounts with bulk purchase for educational, business, or sales promotional use. For information, please write to: Special Sales Department, Andrews McMeel Publishing, 4520 Main Street, Kansas City, Missouri 64111.

Contents

part one

what we fear

being rejected

growing older

failing

being overwhelmed

not being enough

being too much

being loved

being seduced

being betrayed

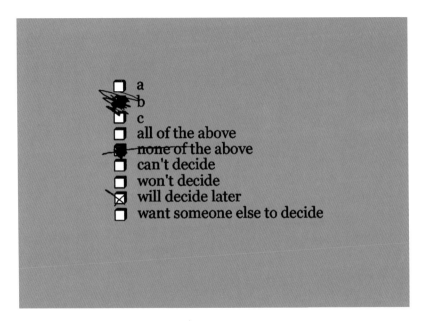

☐ a
◼ b
☑ c
☐ all of the above
◼ none of the above
☐ can't decide
☐ won't decide
☒ will decide later
☐ want someone else to decide

choices

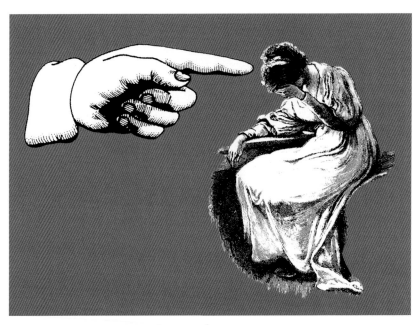

taking the blame

being a fool

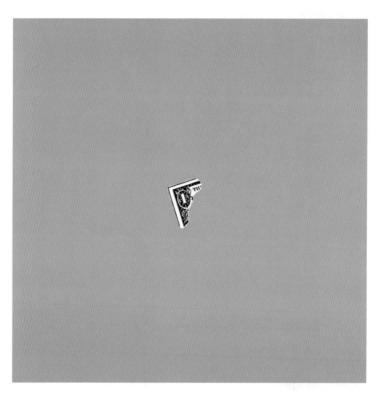

not having enough money

not having enough time

being trapped

being free

being helpless

18

being judged

being lonely

loss

change

responsibility

the unknown

having no control

death

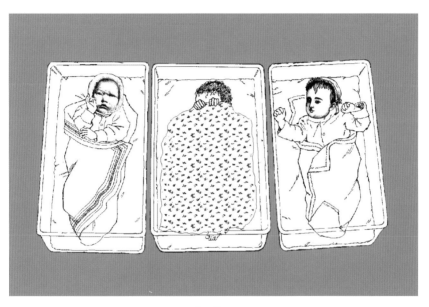

life

part two

how we avoid dealing with our fears

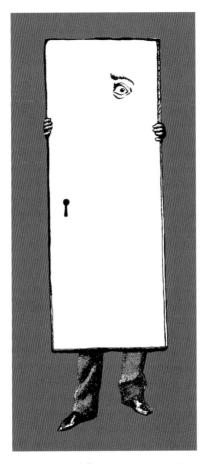

we keep them hidden

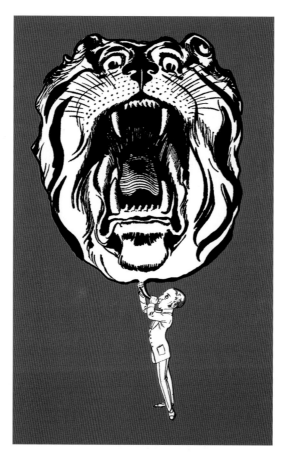

we inflate them

we drown them in various addictions

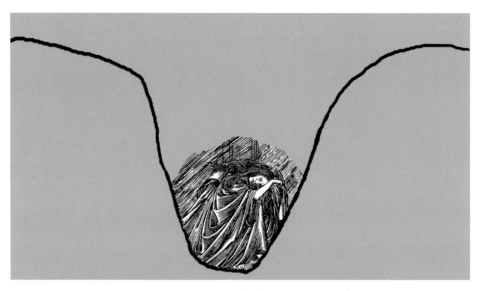

we fall into a depression

we blame others

we live in fantasy

we stay busy

part three

why we avoid dealing with our fears

we can't bear to see our weaknesses

we are too involved with our image

we don't know how to ask for help

we prefer not to grow

we are looking to be saved

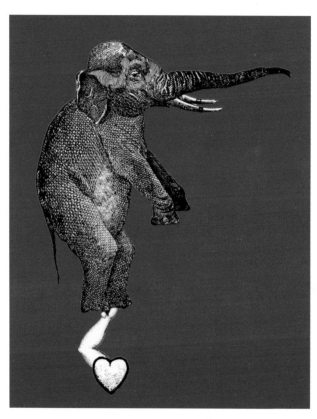

we don't exercise our true strength

we don't think we are ready for change

part four

how we begin dealing with our fears

we muster the courage to face them

we begin to wrestle with them

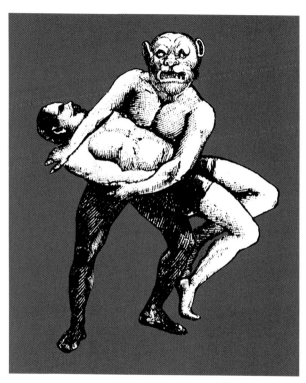

sometimes we may fail

we don't beat ourselves up for it

we call for assistance when needed

we hang on to our sense of humor

part five
helpful hints

courage is not the absence of fear

welcome a challenge

have faith in yourself

stop playing the victim

change your perspective

see <u>all</u> of life as a great adventure

trust that it all happens for a reason

part six

dares

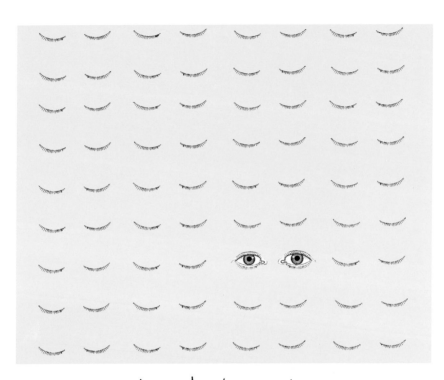

dare to be awake

dare to be yourself

dare to stay calm

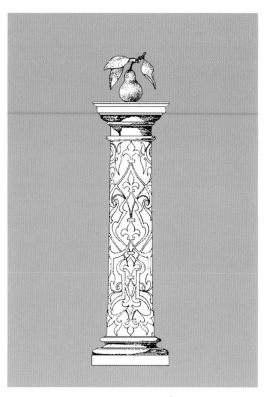

dare to appreciate simple things

dare to celebrate growing older

dare to express yourself

dare to go your own way

part seven
double dares

dare to go deeper

dare to meet your shadow

dare to forgive

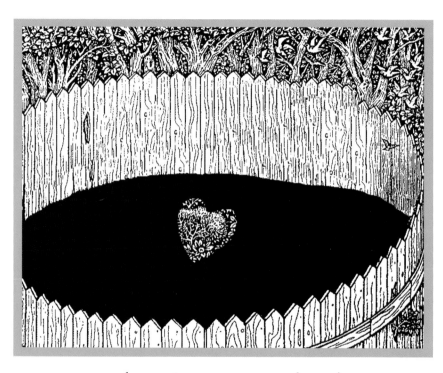

dare to open your heart

dare to be humbled

dare to lend a hand

dare to dance with the mystery of life